GET UP
WITH
SOMETHING ON
YOUR MIND!
Lessons for Navigating Life

A *Gemstones for Living* Book

Howard G. Adams, Ph.D.

Printed in the United States of America:
ISBN No. 0-9705721-2-3

Dedication

This book is dedicated to the life and memory of my parents Daniel Boone Adams (1905 - 1985) and Delsia May Waller Adams (1909-1992). Because of their love, zest for life, values, insight, and faith in tomorrow, I stand tall.

Acknowledgments

The inspiration for this book was kindled by the spoken and written words of many outstanding role models in my life such as the great thinkers, educators and authors Dr. Lyman B. Brooks, Dr. Benjamin E. Mays, Dr. Samuel DeWitt Proctor and Dr. Howard Thurman. For their shining examples of lives of courage, humility and service, I am forever grateful.

While I wrote the text content, I would record my special thanks to the many persons from whose works I quoted in this volume.

Many thanks are offered also to Roxanne Gay for editorial suggestions and comments and Diane Reeder for handling final editing and production. Their assistance was invaluable and much appreciated.

Finally, I would like to thank my wife Dr. Eloise Davis Adams; daughter Dr. Stephanie Glenn Adams; and other family members, friends, and colleagues who have provided encouragement and love over the years.

Preface

Too many times, people look outside themselves to find out what they must do to be successful. We turn to others—parents, significant others, friends, associates, ministers, teachers, counselors, mentors—in search of a success "magic potion" or "hidden secret."

We fail to ask the most important questions:
- Who am I?
- Where am I headed?
- Where do I really want to go with my life?
- Am I ready to take responsibility for the choices I must make?
- What price am I willing to pay?

At the base of it, success begins with YOU.

This book offers a course of action that will help you navigate a successful life. It is a series of lessons, or road maps, for making choices—choices that will determine actions that will ultimately make up the whole of your life.

Feel free to skip around and read what you need when you need it. If you have suggestions on other LESSONS or on how to expand on those developed here, please let me know. Also, listed within the text are numerous quotes and phrases. To maximize their value, internalize those that have special meaning for you and that serve to motivate and drive you onward.

I welcome candid reviews or comments on how the book helped you.

I'd love to hear from you. This book is, itself, in evolution because we all are. If you have lessons you'd like to share, please feel free to send them. With your permission, they may just end up in another book in this series.

Because learning how to navigate through life is a lifelong process, indeed.

Here is how to contact me:

Howard G. Adams, Ph.D.
P.O. Box 7495
Marietta, GA 30065
e-mail: hadamsasso@aol.com

Gemstones for Living
Contents

Introduction

I was born on Adams land, land that my father's father bought in Virginia at the turn of the last century. My grandfather, Jude Adams got it honest: his father, my great-grandpa Ben Adams, was the first Black man on Dan River to own a horse after slavery. My father followed their example, buying more land, an additional farm, when I was eight years old. All in all, we ended up with approximately 200 acres of land—much of which is still in my family today.

The Adams men had something on their mind every day when they woke up. They had land to work, children to raise, a business to run, families to hold together. Growing up, I had 15 aunts and uncles, 60 first-cousins. When we get together in Bachelors Hall, Virginia for our bi-annual family reunion, more than 400 people come.

My dad was the neighborhood elder. When people got in trouble, they came to see him. We'd always know when it was serious. If they took the short walk, there wasn't much to worry about. If they took the long walk, we knew it was serious. "Get up with something on your mind!" he would always tell me. I tried to follow his advice.

I followed it in college, when I went to work bagging groceries wearing creased dress pants and newly-shined shoes. What was on my mind then was that I didn't want to get caught being asked to mop floors. When I did, I'd tell them, "Don't you see my shoes? I can't mop floors in these!"

It worked.

And it worked during my undergraduate days at Norfolk State, the college I attended in Virginia. What was on my mind was that I couldn't afford some of the luxuries of college life—like dorm living. So I slept on a sofa bed at my Auntie Maggie L. Waller's house five blocks from campus. Took it down every night and put it up every morning.

Today, nobody asks me, "Say, where did you sleep when you attended Norfolk State?"

In college, what was on my mind was that I needed to know something. So I went to ballets, debates, speeches, book discussions. I tried to soak up every experience that college offered. And today, nobody knows what I had to go through to get through Norfolk State. They just know that I now have a Bachelor's and Master's, in biology, and the Ph.D. degree in higher education.

What was on my mind was that I could really use a Ph.D. degree. But to get it, I had to commit to work six years in the public schools. Some today might call that a punishment. But for me, it was simply a great training ground for what I would eventually do with my life.

In 1978, I came to this school in Indiana known as the University of Notre Dame. Some people there had heard of my work setting up a national alumni association at Norfolk State, and they asked me to come up north and help launch a program to recruit and graduate students with graduate degrees in engineering. I went to stay five years, and ended up staying eighteen.

Those were great years. We started with eight employers who agreed to support the effort by providing fellowships and internships for twenty-five underrepresented minority engineering graduate students at fourteen universities. We gave it the acronym "GEM," to communicate the precious value these students had to our society. We needed engineers and scientists then, and we still need them today

Eighteen years later, GEM (which stands for The National Consortium for Graduate Degrees for Minorities in Engineering & Science, Inc.) boasted ninety corporate and national governmental laboratory sponsors, including many Fortune 500 companies; seventy-seven universities, including some of the nation's most prominent public and private institutions; and five-hundred students. We saw the annual budget climb from $400,000 to $4 million.

But even more importantly, we saw the vast majority of these students graduate. It's really futile to bring students into a program only to see them drop out before they get the gold. At GEM, that didn't happen.

It didn't happen because we specifically planned for it not to happen: in the way we recruited, in the support we provided throughout the process, in the ways we found to motivate these promising, bright students that they owed it to themselves and to the society to finish, and finish strong.

It didn't happen because we made sure that our corporate and university partners saw themselves as true partners. We showed them that they had just as much of a stake in the success of this effort as any of us. They sat on the board, and they never left. Not a lot of programs can say that.

Not only that, but many of the students we were able to support and nurture have come full circle, to head some of our most prestigious engineering organizations and to work as mentors in their companies and universities; and to come back to their alma maters as top-ranking corporate leaders and tenured professors to encourage other students as they were once encouraged.

And now, I have an opportunity to do what I most love: motivate students to excel first and foremost, but also to give back as good as they have received.

As we move and function in the streams of life, its currents bring us gifts. Some of my most cherished gifts are the wise and thoughtful words of my parents, Daniel Boone Adams and Delsia Mae Waller Adams. When I wake each day, my father's and mother's words sound the challenge that drives me; helping me to focus my life and keep me motivated.

Dad -

"Get up with something on your mind."

"Get up, put your feet on the floor. Wash your face and brush your teeth. Put your clothes on and come downstairs to breakfast. You won't know how you feel until you get up."

"Learn how to meet people."

"The good you do will come back to you."

…and my Mother -

"Your best is good enough."

"Mind your manners."

"I love you."

"Tomorrow will be better than today."

They had other things to say as well, things that have anchored me to this day. Now with a 37-year marriage and two successful women in my life to celebrate (wife Eloise Davis Adams, Ph.D. and daughter Stephanie Glenn Adams, Ph.D. engineering professor) and much ahead to look forward to, I am finally attempting to put their golden gifts into words.

In this book, I share these treasures and others from the streams of my life. As you begin the journey through these lessons, think about the influential people in your own life and the GEMSTONES they have offered you. These GEMSTONES are lessons that I hope will serve as trail markers to help you navigate your way. They are especially aimed at the young at heart; those who will follow and must find their own place to take root, grow, develop, flower and become.

I hope that you, too, will find in these words something to hold on to, so that you will also one day be able to celebrate a rich, full and giving life.

"Do not pray for an easy life. Pray to be a strong person."
-SOURCE UNKNOWN

Life is a struggle.
- Staying alive is a struggle.
- Succeeding in life is a struggle.
- Getting ahead is a struggle.

Indeed, living is a struggle.
-DR. HOWARD G. ADAMS

Lesson I:
Make Right Choices

Question #1: What Do I Dream of Becoming?

Choice:

1. The act of choosing; selection.
2. The power, right, or liberty to choose; option.
3. One that is chosen.
4. A number or variety from which to choose: a wide choice of styles and colors.
5. The best or most preferable part.
6. Care in choosing.
7. An alternative.

Your life is a finite series of moments with an infinite array of choices. Small choices, like what to wear. Life-determining choices, like who to marry or where to work.

As true as this is, we still, as a rule, don't pay enough attention to our own details. We just "let life happen" to us instead of thinking through how to plan and how to decide among the choices available.

Living is about making choices. It involves determining life's possibilities, and then deciding from among those what is probable. To do this takes courage—a boldness to face life through one's personal prism of hope and despair, joy and sadness, confidence and doubt, success and failure. Living demands tenacity—a will to take the hard climb.

Question #2: What price am I willing to pay for the goals I have set for myself?

STEP, STEP, STEP

It has been said that "a journey of a thousand miles begins with a single step." Allow me to propose three important steps for you to take on the journey toward a successful life.

> *Responsibility is the other side of privilege.*
> - MYLES MUNROE, *Noted Speaker/Author*

STEP ONE: Step **Up**

Step up and take responsibility for those factors over which you have control - attitude, time, behavior.

> *Attitude* - Of all the factors which can impact the direction of one's life, attitude is a major determining element. The old adage is true, "attitude determines altitude." Indeed, my favorite play on the acronym "GPA" is, "Govern Your Personal Attitude!"

> *Time* – Your use of time will determine your success. Benjamin Franklin said it best when he said, "do not squander time, for this is the stuff life is made of." Using time wisely is essential to a productive life.

> *Behavior* - Actions do speak louder than words. Personal conduct and decorum in daily activities speak volumes about

your character and provides testimony for defining the quality of that individual.

STEP TWO: Step **Out**
Step out from the crowd. Separate yourself from those who have chosen a path that leads nowhere. Discard those activities, habits, associates, and friends that distract you from concentrating on your goals. Get rid of things and actions that drain your energy but yield little or no return on your investment of time and resources. Shed habits and behaviors that are destructive to your body, your mind, or your spirit.

Stepping out will require courage: courage to be different; courage to function outside the crowd; courage to be your own person.

Dr. Preston Bradley, longtime minister of People's Church in Chicago, said:

"Blessed is the individual who has made up his mind to be himself; who is not going to pattern himself after the media of society..., but is willing to be in the revolution of life. It is a great moment in the life of a person when they discover the integrity of their own inner personality; it's a great moment in the life of a person when they become a personality–not an individual–a personality. It is a great moment when you find the courage to be yourself."

I think Dr. Bradley was saying that we need courage to step out.

Question #3: Do I have the courage to "step out?"

STEP THREE: Step **Onward**
To step onward implies futuristic thinking—to look beyond the moment and visualize future possibilities. It implies optimism and hope. Without optimism and hope, the future is a void in time, with no luster and little to offer in the way of a challenge.

Success in anything starts with a dream, a vision of what the future holds. So you must step onward by holding true to your dreams. For in the words of Langston Hughes, "...if dreams die, life is a broken winged bird that can not fly."

THE STREAMS OF LIFE

At the core of life is a hard purposefulness, a determination to live... Life is alive...life is synonymous with vitality...Life where ever it is found is try-ing to live itself out; to actualize its unique potential.

- DR. HOWARD THURMAN
Minister/Theologian/Author

Life is a stream in search of the sea. During its headlong journey, a stream winds many turns, traverses many obstacles, joins many tribu-taries as it rushes onward to the sea. So it is with life. Life ebbs and flows; we overcome obstacles, experience success and failure, are touched and joined by other lives; and yet, each life rushes onward to its own destiny.

The choices you make will determine how well you navigate the streams of your life, and what effect your stream will have on the rest of the seas of life.

Lesson II:
Plan for success

*Only when you know where you want to go
can you find a route to get there.*

Suc·cess:
1. The achievement of something desired, planned, or attempted.
2. a. The gaining of fame or prosperity.
   b. The extent of such gain.
3. One that is successful.

Question #4: Do I know where I want to go?

When Alice was trying to decide which way to go during her travels, she asked the Cheshire cat, "Would you tell me, please, which way I ought to go from here?" "That depends a good deal on where you want to go," replied the cat. "I don't much care," said Alice. "Then it doesn't matter which way you go," said the cat. The message of the story is clear: only when you know where you want to go can you find a route to get you there.

For some people life is haphazard and inconsistent. That's simply because their "life-goal" planning is haphazard and inconsistent. "Those who fail to plan, plan to fail." That's true in your educational life, your professional life, and your personal and spiritual life.

What is "life-goal planning?" It is a way to chart a course for getting where you want to go. It is a systematic approach to identifying and clarifying your dreams, aspirations, desires and needs.

The focus of life-goal planning is self-determination. It offers you a constructive and realistic method for establishing goals and mapping strategies for accomplishing them

> **LIFE PRINCIPLE:** Planning is a process, not an event.

A plan for any part of your life should include goals (what you want), and action steps (strategies for getting you there).

List your goals and dreams – several for each phase of your life. Make sure you write your goals and action steps down. More often than not what is written down is accomplished. Goals give direction.

Question #5: What are the things that are most important to me?

A well-designed plan that contains focused goals accomplishes these critical things:

- Helps you recognize what needs to be done.
- Encourages you to identify obstacles and use a problem solving approach.
- Helps identify sources of information.
- Encourages discipline.
- Helps you analyze choices.
- Forces you to clarify what you really want to do.
- Encourages opportunism.
- Causes you to act, to stop procrastinating.

- Prepares you to accept responsibility for your life and the choices you make.
- Mobilizes your energy.
- Gets you deeply involved with your own success.
- Organizes your behavior toward achieving your goals.

> **LIFE PRINCIPLE:** Goals have to be nurtured, regularly assessed and acted upon.

Question #6: Do I have a road map?

Goals have to be nurtured, regularly assessed and acted upon. Once you have identified your goals, you must map strategies – an action plan – for accomplishing them. An action plan is a declaration of intent; an "I will" statement that spells out what is to be done with a completion date:

I will   (goal to be accomplished) _____

_____

by (date for accomplishment) _____

Next, map out strategies to identify both opportunities and challenges along the path towards achieving your goals. In so doing, you will be in a better position to choose from the available options.

A written plan provides the blueprint for charting a course of action. It gives you control over your life—at least over the things that you are able to control.

Question #7: What small thing will I do today to make sure I move toward that which is important to me?

Lesson III:
Function with a PURPOSE

Get up with something on your mind.
- DANIEL BOONE ADAMS

Pur·pose:
1. The object toward which one strives or for which something exists; an aim or a goal.
2. A result or effect that is intended or desired; an intention.
3. Determination; resolution.
4. The matter at hand; the point at issue.

"Get up with something on your mind!" My dad challenged me with that line more than fifty years ago, and it is a line that I will always remember. It was a constant challenge from my father for us Adams family members to live purposefully and positively in any circumstance.

To dad, if you started each day with a purpose, things would usually go well. If, however, you started the day without motive or willpower, you could only expect a so-so day.

Fifty years later I can still hear my father's challenge to "Get up, the day is wasting away!" He didn't want to hear, "Daddy, I don't feel well." If he did, he'd simply reply, "Get up, put your feet on the floor, wash your face and brush your teeth. You won't know how you feel until you get up."

Dad instilled in us the need to have a purpose for our lives. "If you have fertile ground for a garden, but don't plant any seeds, the sun and rain will produce weeds," he'd tell us. "But if your purpose is to grow a garden and you follow through by planting, cultivating and nurturing the plants, you should expect a good harvest."

Successful people have an aura of success about them; they look successful, they act successful, they associate with successful people. They function with a purpose.

Purpose means having a focal point for your life. It implies developing your own way of centering your life around something worthwhile. It gives depth and dimension to your life. It will allow you to bring the various phases of your total being together so that you can hold steady and true and keep on course.

Lesson IV:
Maintain a success-oriented mind-set

Mind·set:

1. A fixed mental attitude or disposition that predetermines a person's responses to and interpretations of situations.
2. An inclination or a habit.

When I was teaching at a junior high-school in Virginia, I discovered a program that would pay for my Master's degree—but only if I was willing to drive 85 miles every Saturday to Virginia State University for the classes.

I had the desire, but it was not enough. I had to be willing to make that sacrifice every weekend for the four years it would take to secure that goal.

> **LIFE PRINCIPLE:** Success is operating in the midst of your purpose.

A success-oriented mind-set implies a certain attitude. *Desire* alone is not enough; it must also be accompanied by *determination* and *dedication*—what I often refer to as the "3Ds." Your potential to succeed depends almost exclusively on that 3-part attitude.

But even more than that, you will have to define what "winning" means. Will it mean simply "beating the other guy"—a "winner take all" attitude? If that's all winning means to you, you're in for a rude awakening. Winning doesn't just mean competing with others. It means brainstorming with others, negotiating with others, and teaming with others toward a common goal.

Question #8: What are the roadblocks that keep me from winning?

There are three major factors that prevent most people from developing and maintaining a mind-set for success.

Fear of failure. Time after time people fail by not trying; by giving up before starting; by expecting to fail. Some people approach life with a defeatist attitude – "I can't!" "I couldn't possibly do that!" "I would fail!" People who take that route are on a downward spiral toward their own low expectations. They run from any activity that even looks like success, and so create self-fulfilling prophecies.

Giving in to negative labels. As you move through your life, negative labels can and do become barriers that pigeonhole you and thus become limiting factors.

Negative Labels

* lack creativity
* too detailed
* not a leader
* low profile

* non-risk taker
* lack confidence
* can't inspire
* is more an observer

Question #9: Which roadblocks come from inside me, and which come from other people?

Labels like these create low expectations for both the labeler and the labeled. They diminish a person's perceived quality, and contribute to personal insecurity, fear and anxiety. To overcome this and build self-esteem, ask yourself these questions instead:

- Who am I?
- What are my attributes?
- What are my strengths/weaknesses?
- What do I want for myself?

Strengthening your resolve to succeed will start when you develop a mind-set to address and shed negative labels.

Looking to others for approval. A restrained mind-set—one that is always waiting for permission to act, to move, to take charge, to become—imprisons a person. Noted author and theologian Dr. Howard Thurman called this "being the enemy in one's own skin."

Success is more than a mere word; it is a way of life. It is embodied by the way you feel about yourself, your opportunities, your options, and your ability to identify and make choices.

A success-oriented mind-set involves developing those behaviors, attitudes, beliefs, values, and habits to: 1) desire success; 2) feel worthy of success; 3) have the will to succeed; and one more thing: 4) possess the courage to enjoy your success. Some people, despite all they have accomplished, keep a tape running in their heads of every negative thing that others have said. They have so internalized these negative self-concepts that nothing they do will ever be good enough for them. It takes courage to throw out those internal tapes and dare to enjoy the things you have accomplished.

Question #10: Which roadblocks can I change?

Lesson V:
Start with hard work

The only place that success comes before work is in the dictionary.
- DR. PATRICIA RUSSELL MCCLOUD, *Noted Speaker*

Work:
1. Physical or mental effort or activity directed toward the production or accomplishment of something.
2. a. A job; employment.
   b. A trade, profession, or other means of livelihood.
3. a. Something that one is doing, making, or performing, especially as an occupation or undertaking; a duty or task..
   b. An amount of such activity either done or required: a week's work.
4. Something that has been produced or accomplished through the effort, activity, or agency of a person or thing.

Are you willing to pay the price for the success that you say you are looking for? Then get ready to work.

That's the bottom line. Work—your own personal initiative—is the one thing that you can control regardless of your individual circumstances, surroundings, or influences.

Work is a wholesome activity. It activates the spirit and mobilizes it into energy to accomplish a specific task.

In all my talks with young people, I challenge them with the statement, "opportunity means nothing without effort; you must apply yourself." I call this application of effort my 3T's - time on task using your talents.

> *The reward of a thing well done is to have done it.*
> - RALPH WALDO EMERSON, *Author/Philosopher*

Do you want to be seen as a professional, someone who is proficient, productive, and committed to quality? If so, you must demonstrate those qualities. If so, you must see work as honorable.

Work is satisfying. The joy of work done well is the personal satisfaction that comes with the acknowledgment that "I did that and it is good!" Don't spend your time pleasing others with your work. Please yourself through excellent performance.

Work is rewarding even beyond the personal satisfaction of a job well done. Test this theory: try working to the level of the high standards you have set for yourself. Then watch as the other, external rewards—pay, recognition, accolades—accrue to you as well.

Work makes success possible. Myles Munroe in his book, *Releasing your Potential*, says, "Potential is the existence of possibilities. Work is the activation of possibilities."

Striving to succeed through hard work puts your attributes—energy, skills, knowledge, initiative—to good use as you activate your plans.

Question #11: What rewards am I looking for in my work?

Lesson VI:
Aim high

It must be borne in mind that the tragedy of life doesn't lie in not reaching your goal, the tragedy lies in having no goal to reach. It isn't a disaster to be unable to capture your ideals, but it is a disaster to have no ideal to capture. It's not a disgrace not to reach the stars, but it is a dis - grace to have no stars to reach for. Not failure, but low aim, is a sin.

- Dr. Benjamin E. Mays
Former Morehouse College
President, Minister, Author

Aim:
1. To direct toward or intend for a particular goal or group.
2. To determine a course or direct an effort: aim for a better education.
3. To propose to do something; intend.

What is your dream for your life? Where do you want to live? How do you want to live? Married? Single? Children? What do you want to be your life's work? And most importantly, how high is your aim?

You must aim directly, and you must aim high, and you must aim higher as you progress through life. If your high aim seems unattainable, don't worry: better to aim high and hit a little lower than to aim low and hit bottom.

Others may judge you foolish. "You dream too big," they might say. "You'll never be able to do that; it's a million-to-one shot." Does that bother you? Then don't talk to them. Don't let them define or limit or confine you to their own preconceived notions. Instead, get busy on planning and working to make your dreams a reality.

Question #12: How willing am I to have others define for me my station in life?

Also: dream a little. Dreams help you paint a picture of what you want for yourself. Just as important as hard work is envisioning where you want to be; it motivates you to walk toward that dream.

But aiming high involves more than just dreaming. It involves strategy and adaptation. It involves knowing what road to take. It involves understanding the sacrifices, the obstacles, and the rewards. It involves understanding.

So: Aim high. Ignore other people's low expectations. Know the price required, adapt to the obstacles, and strategize.

Finally: enjoy the rewards!

Lesson VII:
Take advantage of opportunity

Opportunity will knock, but it does not pick a lock.
- COACH EARL EUBANKS

Op·por·tu·ni·ty:

1. A favorable or advantageous circumstance or combination of circumstances.
2. A favorable or suitable occasion or time.
3. A chance for progress or advancement.

The most successful people are those who look for opportunity in every facet of their lives.

How do other successful people identify, evaluate, and act upon the opportunities and options available to them? They follow some of these key strategies. Take a look and see which ones you have embraced as your own. For those you have not yet mastered, write just one thing you will do under each one to get started:

Strategy   What I Will Do

- plan for success   _____
- establish success goals   _____
- practice discipline   _____
- manage priorities wisely _____

- use time wisely   _____
- avoid activities that drain
  energy without any rewards   _____
- exhibit success habits   _____
- have self-confidence   _____
- associate with successful
  people   _____
- plan to be the best   _____
- play the game to win, in
  every sense of the word   _____
- understand power   _____
- maintain persistence   _____
- accept challenges as
  opportunities   _____
- take risks   _____
- network   _____
- work hard   _____
- work smart   _____
- be productive   _____
- expect and accept change   _____
- find a mentor   _____

Although "opportunity will knock," there is usually a limited window to act. My own mentor, Dr. Lyman B. Brooks, as President of Norfolk State University, would remind the student body, "opportunity runs hard and fast and you must seize it as it approaches. For once it passes, you lose the moment, and it may never come again."

When you take advantage of opportunities wherever they present themselves, you become more optimistic about the future. You're more likely to seek, explore and evaluate options. And you will find that you will always be prepared when the opportunity comes.

Question #13: Am I ready?

Lesson VIII:
Be willing to take risks

There are essentially four kinds of risks:
The risk one must accept.
The risk one can afford to take.
The risk one cannot afford to take
The risk one cannot afford not to take.
    — DR. PETER DRUCKER, *Business Consultant/Author*

Risk :
1. The possibility of suffering harm or loss; danger.
2. A factor, thing, element, or course involving uncertain danger; a hazard.
3. The variability of returns from an investment.

Have you ever said, "I wish I had done that, but I was scared I might fall on my face?" Many people are afraid to fail, afraid to take even a moderate risk in order to take advantage of a great opportunity. Conversely, many an opportunity has been lost because of risking too much. Play it too safe and you may lose; gamble wildly and you may lose.

Most people don't venture into the unknown because they fear failure. They rationalize their fears by finding fault with the new situation — "it's bad timing; it's the wrong location; it might hurt the family."

Being a risk taker means being audacious; being bold and daring enough to move beyond the safety of the harbor. Being a risk taker means you are willing and daring enough to venture into the deep waters of life.

Get off the sidelines; there is nothing there for you. Weigh and consider the risk, and decide whether it's worth it. If it is, go for it! You just never know...

Question #14: Am I willing to take the risks that will lead to success?

Lesson IX:
Accept delayed gratification

"You bet I arrived (to success) overnight. Over a few hundred nights in the Catskills, in vaudeville, in clubs and on Broadway.."
— DANNY KAYE, *Entertainer*

Gratification:

1. The act of gratifying, or pleasing, either the mind, the taste, or the appetite; as, the gratification of the palate, of the appetites, of the senses, of the desires, of the heart.
2. That which affords pleasure; satisfaction; enjoyment; fruition: delight.
3. A reward; a recompense; a gratuity.

Success is not instant. It doesn't pop up like microwave popcorn or come in ready-to-eat packages. The notion of instant success is a fantasy. The supposedly overnight success stories are few, and when you pull the covers back, you'll find that most of even those stories involved serious behind-the-scenes planning and dedicated effort.

Some battles can be easily won, but others take time, determination, and stick-to-itiveness. The laws of nature hold that an object at rest will remain at rest until acted on by some outside force. The outside force that causes you to act is the combination of your desires, dreams and fortitude.

Successful people in all walks of life, be they athletes, farmers, entertainers, politicians, cooks, doctors, lawyers, assembly workers, plumbers, secretaries, parents, teachers—or students—pay a high price for their success—the price of training, time, energy, and sacrifice. The rewards are not always immediate. Be patient. Expect and accept delayed gratification. And remember to enjoy the journey.

Success is a journey, not a destination.
- AUTHOR UNKNOWN

Question #15: How long am I willing to wait to become an "overnight success?"

Lesson X:
Respect your potential

...it must not be thought that life is static, fixed, determined. The key word to remember always is potential: that which has not yet come to pass but which is always coming to pass. It is only potential, the undisclosed, the unfinished that has a future.

- DR. HOWARD THURMAN

Po·ten·tial:
1. The inherent ability or capacity for growth, development, or coming into being.
2. Something possessing the capacity for growth or development.

When I got to Norfolk State University, I heard what college students often hear: "Look to the right and to the left. In four years, one of you is not going to be here." What an awful way for leaders in higher administration to introduce new students to college!

That practice still happens sometimes, and you need to know the right response. When I heard that dire sentence, I told people: "I am a Virginia gentleman (a gentleman was one whose family owned land); I am worthy to be here. And not only am I staying, I have cousins who are coming behind me." Sometimes, it's okay to directly confront those who would rather not see you there.

Often people fail to realize their full potential because they do not respect and believe in themselves. If you don't think you're worthy, you won't belong—not because of any inadequacies on your part, but because people will reflect back to you what you see in yourself. A lack of respect for your own personal worth, unique value, and ability to make a contribution will determine your level of achievement.

Cease to be a drudge; seek to be an artist.
-MARY MCLEOD BETHUNE, *Educator*

How can you come to a place where you respect your own potential? Is it enough to tell yourself over and over again, "I belong, I belong, I belong?" That may help, but the best remedy for overcoming a lack of respect for one's own potential is a dogged determination not to accept the ordinary. Don't allow yourself to develop a "that'll do" attitude. Don't accept an ordinary performance of yourself. Strive to be extraordinary.

Living is about following one's hopes and dreams. It's about reaching and striving. It's about becoming. It's about trying to realize your potential—all that you are and hope to be.

Say to yourself, "That which is in me is always in the process of becoming. I have potential. I have ability."

Don't let others convince you otherwise.

Question #16: What is in me that I need to nurture, bring out, and show the world?

Lesson XI:
Value education*

Education is that which remains when one has forgotten everything he (she) learned in school.
- ALBERT EINSTEIN

Ed·u·ca·tion:

1. The act or process of educating or being educated.
2. The knowledge or skill obtained or developed by a learning process.
3. A program of instruction of a specified kind or level.
4. The field of study that is concerned with the pedagogy of teaching and learning.
5. An instructive or enlightening experience.

Education is life. When a person is born, education begins, when they die, education ends. To appreciate life is to appreciate and value education. To neglect life is to fail to understand that the nature of education is ongoing.

It is also important to recognize that education takes place both inside and outside of the classroom. You can learn from anyone: parents, siblings, friends, bosses, educators, peers—and not-so-peers.

Education is a freeing experience. It enables you to ask intelligent questions and explore the unknown. In the words of Dr. Benjamin E.

Mays, "education stirs you up." It provides the will to push hard on those closed doors to new frontiers.

Education is freedom. It frees the mind and spirit. It allows you to experience new and challenging horizons without boundaries, or walls: walls of FEAR; walls of SUPERSTITIONS; walls that make individual achievement seem IMPOSSIBLE. These walls chain the human spirit and narrow horizons. They stifle creativity, cloud vision and create self-appointed "second-class citizens."

You can be educated and not be free; but you cannot be free without education. Education frees the human spirit.

Question #17: What will I do to educate myself?

* Adapted from a speech by the author, "The Quality of Education and Freedom", Honors Convocation, Winston Salem State University, Winston Salem, N.C., 1991.

Lesson XII:
Maintain your values

Without values, you lose your way, and if you lose your way, all is lost.
— MRS. FANNIE GRIGGS CLARK, *Bible School Teacher*

Val·ue:
1. Monetary or material worth.
2. Worth in usefulness or importance to the possessor; utility or merit.
3. A principle, standard, or quality considered worthwhile or desirable.

Values define you. They determine who you are, how you act, who you associates with; what you care about.

Mrs. Fannie Griggs Clark in Summer Bible School provided one of my early lessons on values. She taught in Griggs Chapel, a small country chapel named after her father, Mr. William Griggs, a distinguished and charismatic man who could have easily been a senator or a judge had he not been born when he was born—or had he been born another color. He managed to acquire a stately house on 100 acres of land, and made a name for himself within his community.

Mrs. Clark was slightly built; she smoked, and drove fast, and talked fast. She took us places we might not have otherwise gone, and always made sure that we behaved. Children even today know of her reputation because their parents and grandparents have repeated her story over and over.

"Don't be like Esau, who sold his birthright for a mess of pottage," Mrs. Clark would tell us. In that small country chapel, she let us know that certain things could not be measured in dollars and cents, that we should never get to a place where we could be bought. She let us know that values were the very essence of each of us—all that we were and all that we would later become. She encouraged us to hold true to our values and keep family traditions alive. She warned us that "without values, you lose your way, and if you lose your way, all is lost."
Your values will keep, sustain, and fortify you when nothing else will.

Keep your way lit with the values you learned in your youth.

Question #18: Who and what do I value?

Lesson XIII:
Learn from your experiences

Experience is the best teacher.
- SOURCE UNKNOWN

Ex·pe·ri·ence:
1. The apprehension of an object, thought, or emotion through the senses or mind.
2. Active participation in events or activities, leading to the accumulation of knowledge or skill and the knowledge or skill so derived.
3. An event or a series of events participated in or lived through and the totality of such events in the past of an individual or group.

Your experiences, whether "successes" or "failures," give you a chance to learn, grow and develop. As you move through life, you will frequently find yourself on uncharted seas: daunting and unexpected challenges, new situations, new people, new and difficult tasks. Handle these challenges successfully, and you will develop new skills and acquire new, positive attitudes about your abilities. These "irritants" can bring out hidden talents, polish existing talents and build confidence. They are like the sand in the oyster that brings shape and sheen to the pearl inside.

When I graduated from high school, I went north–the East Coast–to expore, to experience something different. When I came back south to attend college, the only job I could find was bagging groceries. It was a menial job, but I decided I would perform my duties with a high degree of professionalism and dignity. I became a "professional" bag boy, making sure my appearance was impeccable. I put a knife-crease in my pants every morning and shined my shoes and wore a tie everyday. When my superiors asked me to scrub floors, I would tell them: "See my shiny shoes? I can't scrub the floor in these."

And I learned how to run a store. Not because they gave me any additional responsibilities, but simply by watching how they did it. Because of that experience, I eventually was able to improve my status by becoming a "floating" manager for a fast food chain of six stores. I had decided I wasn't going to let them box me in to one role. If they wouldn't promote my expansion and learning, I would do it myself.

Maximize the value you take from your experiences, regardless of how you may see them. Know that you may frequently experience more failures than successes, and that there are ways for you to cope even with that harsh reality. Here are a few "Do's and Don'ts" for you to remember:

Do:
• develop strong personal, and realistic goals.
• look for positive lessons in your failures.
• possess a sense of empowerment.

Don't:
• look for instant success.
• go it alone.
• berate yourself for "failing."

Question #19: What are the 3 most important lessons I have learned from my experiences?

Lesson XIV:
Form networks

Learn how to meet people.
- *DANIEL BOONE ADAMS*

Networking:
1. The exchange of information or services among individuals, groups, or institutions.

- Networking is contacts.
- Networking is information.
- Networking is ideas and feedback.
- Networking is support.
- Networking is power.

AMY B. TEDDER, *Success* Magazine

My dad taught me very early about the importance of meeting people–in the church, in the community, wherever we went. What he understood at a basic level was the concept we now know as "networking."

The term "networking" came of age in the '80s decade as a way to define the formal and informal exchanges between professionals—exchanges that take place through daily contacts and associations.

Informal networking can occur almost anywhere: eating lunch with a co-worker, talking on a plane to a seat mate, dropping by to talk with a colleague, after work get-togethers. In these mundane but frequent encounters, you can pick up suggestions and strategies, build helpful allies, learn new techniques; and acquire valuable information. You have to be ready in such encounters with a question to ask, some valuable information to share, or some help to offer.

Formal networking mainly occurs through attending professional meetings, conferences, trade shows, and planned meal functions. These and other formal settings provide excellent opportunities to circulate and make contacts.

Networking should not be left to chance; it should be practiced wherever you go. When a contact is made that may be helpful in the future, be sure to follow it up with appropriate notes, letters or phone calls. If someone aided you in making the contact, seek their permission to reference them in the follow-up.

To make the most of networking practices, take time to develop strong relationships with a variety of successful people. Be sure to build strong alliances with associates and contacts in other organizations, companies, and institutions. You can use these alliances to expand your horizons, build credibility, and identify other options and opportunities.

And remember: networking is a two-way street. Be just as willing to give as you are to get, whether it is information, assistance, or resources; and you'll find many more doors will open to you.

Question #20: Whom do I need to meet? What of value can I offer them?

Lesson XV:
Find a mentor

Finding and making use of the right mentor is the
most critical step you'll ever take in your career.
- LINDA PHILLIP-JONES, Educator

Men·tor:
1. A wise and trusted counselor or teacher.

It is difficult trying to go it alone. You need a mentor. Mentors are experienced professionals, whose position, status, and expertise makes them uniquely qualified to: (1) transmit valuable information and knowledge; 2) influence future career opportunities; 3) provide critical feedback; and 4) serve as a "reality check." Mentors are important allies; they can be a teacher, role model, counselor, trusted advisor, advocate, challenger, encourager, sponsor, confidant, coach, or friend. (Howard G. Adams and Stephanie G. Adams, 1993)

Finding and selecting a mentor (or mentors; it is possible and even advisable to have more than one), someone who will take time and make the effort needed to help you craft and carry out your success plan, is a difficult task that should not be taken lightly. Linda Phillip-Jones, in *Mentors and Protégés*, says it this way: "Finding and making use of the right mentor is the most critical step you'll ever take in your career."

Ideally, in seeking and selecting a mentor you will want to identify and choose someone to challenge, coach, teach and sponsor you. You are looking for someone who is willing to work with you to help you shape your goals, implement strategies, and establish you in the most favorable position to succeed.

As you establish a workable mentorship alliance, keep these important DOs and DON'Ts in mind:

- Do move past race and gender in your search for a mentor.
- Do identify your needs and expectations of a mentoring relationship.
- Do work to establish trust between you and your mentor.
- Do develop strategic action steps to act on your mentor's advice.
- Do create a favorable image to prove yourself worthy.

- Don't duck your personal roles and responsibilities.
- Don't create a "me-me" situation - mentoring alliances are symbiotic (shared) relationships.
- Don't take personal critiques and feedback as an attack on you.
- Don't let your ego dominate your actions.
- Don't violate the rules of confidentiality; your breach of confidence is sure to be found out.

Question #21: What person in the community, at school, or on my job can I really learn from?

Lesson XVI:
Find an anchor(s)

An·chor:
1. A rigid point of support, as for securing a rope.
2. A source of security or stability.

The descendents of my paternal grandfather Jube Adams and his first and second wives, Mary and Nellie, have held the Adams' Family Reunion in the Bachelors Hall community of Virginia for more than 80 years in a bi-annual tradition. This tradition, which draws over 400 people—brothers and sisters, aunts and uncles, nieces and nephews, cousins, in-laws, and friends—provides an anchor for the Adams Clan.

At these gatherings, we introduce families, retell history, start new traditions, share good and bad news, and fold love into handshakes, hugs and kisses. Here we rekindle anew, or discover for the first time, what it means to be an Adams, to belong to a family where caring for one another and loving one another is valued and shared. Here the Adams Clan develops anchors that hold hope, provide stability, and fortify.

When I use the term anchor, I speak of those traditions, values, beliefs, and associates that provide fortification, support, connection, and refuge, that allow us to hold steady and true to goals and dreams and to stay on course to mapped plans.

Without anchors, we can be turned off course by the winds of change, moved back and forth by the waves of fear and doubt, ship-wrecked on the sandbars of loneliness and isolation; and even washed out to seas of defeat.

When we develop strong anchors, we "proof" ourselves against the many storms that occur in our lives. Strong anchors help us have courage to overcome our fears, help us to find strength to face and deal with our weaknesses, help us to ride out disappointments, help us handle stresses and anxieties that are a part of our daily lives.

Look for anchors in both your biological family and your chosen family—those friends, lovers, mentors and confidants to whom you turn for love, compassion and support. And be an anchor yourself as you learn to sustain and support others.

We have an anchor that keeps the soul.
- OLD CHRISTIAN HYMN

Question #22: What are the ideals, people, and experiences that have anchored me?

Lesson XVII:
You will get more
Noes than Yeses

When one door...closes, another opens...
- *HELEN KELLER, Educator/Author*

No:
1. Used to express refusal, denial, disbelief, emphasis, or disagreement.
2. Not at all; not by any degree. Often used with the comparative: no better; no more.

In this world there are no guarantees that your desires, recommendations, requests, wishes, or your position on an issue will receive a favorable response. You must be prepared to accept "No!"

People experience major disappointments because they fail to understand that in life you will be told, "No!" Don't take being told "No" as personal rejection; rather, let your competitive instinct spirits kick in to propel your motives and move you to examine why the answer was "No." Ask yourself: "Did I do all I could do?" "Was I convincing?" "In a similar situation, what would my response have been?"

I often tell young people that, when seeking a favor, an opportunity, or in making a request of others, it should be done with the understanding that there are more "noes" than there are "yeses." But "No" does not always mean "No." Many times it simply means, "You didn't give enough information" or "You didn't make the argument convincingly enough." In such cases, "No" is not a defeat, but only a minor setback.

> **LIFE PRINCIPLE:** In a democracy, you are not assured that you will always win, only that you will have the opportunity to participate.

If, after careful examination, you determine that there is hope to turn a "No" into a "Yes," be willing to rework the request and seek others to sanction your efforts. Then, be prepared to make the request again and again. If you still do not prevail, learn to accept "No" as a normal part of the give and take of life. In this life, you are not assured that you will always win, only that you will have the opportunity to participate. And when you take full advantage of that opportunity, you are bound to get to "Yes!"—even if it means that you have to say yes to yourself.

Create your own reality.

Question #23: What are five things I can do to create my own reality?

Lesson XVIII:

"Mind your manners"
- DELSIA MAE WALLER ADAMS

Man·ner:
1. A way of doing something or the way in which a thing is done or happens.
2. A way of acting; bearing or behavior.

Man·ners
1. The socially correct way of acting; etiquette.
2. The prevailing customs, social conduct, and norms of a specific society, period, or group.

As matriarch of a home that was always bustling with the active lives of parents, eight children, numerous visiting relatives, neighbors and friends, my mother kept the young people who were in and out of the house under control with this admonition: "Mind your manners!"

These simple words carried multiple meanings. Depending on the situation, they could mean, "Show respect," or "Watch what you say," or " I don't appreciate how you said something." On other occasions, these words meant, "Check your actions," or "Speak when you are spoken to." In all instances, the warning "Mind your manners!" directed us to be on our best behavior.

Too often in today's society—churches, schools, government forums, workplaces, homes—the admonition to "Mind your manners!" is neither practiced nor transmitted to our youth.

We all need to remember to show respect, watch what is said and how, and be mindful of personal actions when engaged in dialogue and personal contact with others. You'll be surprised how far simple manners take you. It tells people, not just that you read the "etiquette book," but that you care about them and not just yourself.

In an era of rude talk show hosts and guests, angry and impatient drivers, and offensive behavior in every venue, manners are like a breath of fresh air. They can smooth your way to success by making you stand out to your colleagues and superiors.

So, as Delsia Mae Waller Adams (I could never call my mother "Delsia"; I have to say the full name) said: "Mind your manners!"

Question #24: What act of grace can I perform for someone in my life?

Lesson XIX:
Play fair

Do it right the first time and you won't have to apologize.
- HOWARD G. ADAMS

Fair:
1. Having or exhibiting a disposition that is free of favoritism or bias; impartial: a fair mediator.
2. Just to all parties; equitable: a compromise that is fair to both factions.
3. Being in accordance with relative merit or significance.
4. Consistent with rules, logic, or ethics.

During my tenure as a secondary biology/science teacher during the 1960s, the question of fairness occasionally surfaced. Most often the question was raised regarding the interpretation of rules and regulations that governed various interactions: student-to-student, student-to-teacher, student-to-administrative staff. Students' anxieties would be affected most if they perceived that the outcomes from interpreting some rule or regulation appeared to be unfair.

To maintain an open dialogue with my students and to help them develop their own values regarding fairness, I established this philosophical statement for my classroom: "In our dealings with each other, let's do it right the first time and we won't have to apologize." Another practice I instituted was this: at the end of the year, I always let my students grade me. I graded them; why not provide them with the same privilege?

They always responded. And you know? None of the students I failed ever, ever blamed me for their performance. They perceived me as fair, they saw me reciprocate fairness, and they were able to take responsibility for their own actions.

Unfairness can change the way a person looks at the world. It can damage them forever. It makes them react differently, in a way that says to others, "Nothing I do, good or bad, matters anyway. I may as well do nothing—or the wrong thing." We must learn to be fair in all our dealings.

Fairness should be the standard for all relationships—whether they are personal, collegial, pastoral, educational, supervisory, or work-related. The whole concept of fairness demands that where personhood is involved—feelings, pride, options, opportunities, rewards, recognitions—we should always "do it right the first time."

Question #25: Is there anyone with whom I have cut corners in terms of fairness? How can I rectify that?

Lesson XX:
Use what you have

Take what you have and make something out of it.
- GEORGE WASHINGTON CARVER,
Scientist/Inventor/Educator

Have:
1. a. To be in possession of
   b. To possess as a characteristic, quality, or function.
   c. To possess or contain as a constituent part.
2.   To possess knowledge of or facility in.

My friend and undergraduate classmate, Dr. Julian M. Earls, Deputy Director, NASA Lewis Research Center in Cleveland, Ohio, uses a classic story to illustrate how to use what you have. As the story goes (as told by Dr. Earls), a college professor was known to give the same philosophy exam question at the end of each term, "Trace the Wanderings of Moses." Students anticipating this question would memorize Moses' wandering in the wilderness and come ready to take the exam.

The Dean of the College became aware of this practice and ordered the professor to change the question. On the appointed day for the exam, students marched in with their wanderings already memorized only to learn that the question was changed to, "Critique The Lord's Sermon on the Mountain."

Students, after reading the question, one by one, closed their exam blue books and walked out of the class muttering that this was unfair, a trick played on poor helpless students. Finally, all that remained was one student who wrote the whole exam period.

When the professor received this student's exam booklet he was so excited that he opened it immediately to see what the student had written. That student simply wrote, "Who am I to question the Master? As for me, I am going to write about the 'Wanderings of Moses.'"

The professor assigned a grade of "A" to the paper and wrote a footnote, "Thank you for working with what you had."

Some people spend their lives lamenting how life has short-changed them. They whine about how their lives would have been easier, fuller, more rewarding, "If only I had... some of this; more of that; if only I had..." They spend their lives on the sidelines of life, watching the parades go by.

To conclude that "there is nothing I can do, fate has ruled," is to run from life. Indeed, it might have been easier had circumstances or the situation been different. But you must play the hand that is dealt to you.

Remember, not all situations are as bad as they first appear. Within the not-so-favorable situation, one can usually find opportunities to turn coal into diamonds and oysters into pearls by paying attention to the details: planning, assessing goals, and taking specific, well thought-out action steps.

Our ancestors understood this. They didn't have doctors, but they turned plants into delicacies and medicines. They didn't have computers or phones or fax machines, but they found ways to get information to those who needed it.

We can learn from their example. Use what you have.

Question #26: What do I have? How can I use it?

Lesson XXI:
Time is a precious gift

Until you value yourself, you won't value your time. Until you value your time, you will not do anything with it.

                                                                    - M. SCOTT PECK, Author

Time:

1.   To arrange or set the time of; to regulate.
2.   To set the tempo, speed, or duration.
3.   To dispose so that an action occurs at a desired instant or in a desired way.

   Time is a precious gift. But some of us just don't get it. We carelessly or unknowingly fritter away valuable time. Time can be an ally or an enemy.

   For some, this is due to lack of wise planning. For others, it is the failure to follow a schedule, or to make wise use of unproductive empty hours each day. Whatever the reason, poor use of time is a bad habit that will ultimately derail any plans for success you may have.

At best the span of life is short. Our entrances and our exits on the stage of passing time are controlled by a destiny higher than we with our finite minds are permitted to understand. When the hour approaches for the final curtain, there is not time to look back or to try things over again or even to transmit to others the advice of the era, which, having discovered its own mistake, yearns in vain for another chance.

- DAVID LAWRENCE, Author

So what's the answer? Change your habits. A habit is simply anything you do regularly over a period of time. Make it a habit to budget your time. Make it a habit to schedule each day. Make it a habit to use some of your "empty" hours more productively. List high priorities to help keep you focused on important tasks. Here are other suggestions:

Key Strategies for Maximizing Time

- Organize your schedule - take a few minutes at the start of each day to prioritize task.
- Establish a routine for day-to-day tasks and stick to it.
- Keep a log of progress—make notes on work in progress and meet time lines.
- Take time for yourself—allow personal time for rejuvenation and relaxation.

Redeem the time.
- THE BIBLE

Question #27: What are some actions I can take to buy back the time I have lost?

Lesson XXII:
Take charge of your life

May you live all the days of your life.

- JONATHAN SWIFT, Author

Charge:
1. To impose a duty, responsibility, or obligation on.

Success is an individual quest. It is achieved through personal initiative. It flows from the most important personal statement the individual can make: "I will take charge of my life; I will be responsible."

This will take personal commitment, discipline, and initiative. Being disciplined means you are careful with your first steps and consistently build on each step after that. It means doing what you have to do simply because it has to be done.

Discipline and initiative are a direct reflection of your attitude. And who is in charge of your attitude? You! You can take charge of your life.

Here are some simple things that each person can do to take charge:
• Tap into inner powers that you don't now use.

- Stop blaming others.
- Stop seeing yourself as the victim.
- Get a new identity by saying to yourself:
  - I am somebody!
  - Success is possible for me!
  - I control my own destiny!
- Find something you like to do and put your energy to work.

You must always be focused on what you can do for yourself. Start by taking charge of your life.

Question #28: What three affirmations can I say to myself that will help me take charge of my life?

Lesson XXIII
"Read the paper everyday"
- DANIEL BOONE ADAMS

News·pa·per

1: A paper that is printed and distributed usually daily or
     weekly and that contains news, articles of opinion, features,
     and advertising.

My father was a habitual daily reader of the newspaper and he
challenged my siblings and me to do likewise: "You MUST read the
newspaper everyday.... For they might declare war and you won't
know anything about it."

This is one of the lessons from our parents that my four brothers,
three sisters and I have taken to heart. Each of us tries very hard to
start each day by devoting some time to reading a newspaper. When
this is not possible, we have a mandate from our father to do so before
going to bed each night.

That simple, yet profound advice from my father played out its
significance in my life in the 1980s, during the Tylenol tampering
scare. The media declared "war" on Tylenol after it was discovered that
some packages were laced with cyanide.

During the period that the tampering scare was being investigated, I flew into Chicago O'Hare Airport on a United Airlines flight. Upon exiting the plane and entering the airport corridor, I was met with the glaring headline in all the local newspapers: "Don't take Tylenol." A United flight attendant arrived around the same time and in the same corridor, went home without reading the newspaper headlines, took Tylenol and died that night. War had been declared on Tylenol, but because the flight attendant didn't read the newspaper, she lost her life.

I have relayed this true story in many of my personal development seminars and lectures to illustrate the importance of being informed. Living fruitfully and successfully requires being in touch with one's surroundings—locally, nationally and internationally. One important way of keeping abreast of current events is through reading the newspaper everyday.

Lesson XXIV:
"Your best is good enough"
- DELSIA MAE WALLER ADAMS

E·nough
1. Sufficient to meet a need or satisfy a desire; adequate.

As a freshman in college, I came face-to-face with doubt. I had expected college to be very challenging, but not so difficult that I would not be able to cope with the work. My optimism was challenged immediately. With a freshman year course load of seventeen hours including English, chemistry, college algebra, and world history, my ability to handle college academic work became a serious concern and a source of great anxiety.

On a visit home, during the second semester of my freshmen year, I shared these concerns with my mother. After hearing me out, she paused from preparing a pound cake (my favorite), looked me straight in my eyes and asked two questions, "Are you studying as you should? Are you putting forth your best effort?" "Yes mama!" I replied. She turned back to her work and firmly said, "your best is good enough." And then added, "Keep giving it your best; everything will be okay." Those were reassuring words from a mother to her son; words that have served me well throughout my academic and professional life.

My friend and colleague Ted Habarth, Founder of the GEM Program (National Consortium for Graduate Degrees for Minorities in Engineering and Science, Inc.) reminds me often that many young people suffer from an almost daily dosage of being told "Why bother? You're not good enough." Such messages are debilitating, for they zap the spirit, destroy motive, and decimate the will to persevere.

My mother's words, "Your best is good enough," gave me needed encouragement. Her charge "keep giving it your best," provided me the challenge to maintain my effort.

Excellence should be the goal for every endeavor, and achievement the reward. You should never expect or accept anything less than functioning and performing at the highest level of your ability. And always remember…"your best is good enough."

Lesson XXV:
"Tomorrow will be better"
- DELSIA MAE WALLER ADAMS

bet·ter

1. Greater than half.
2. Improved in health or mental attitude.
3. More attractive, favorable, or commendable.
4. More advantageous or effective.
5. Improved in accuracy or performance.

Mother was an optimist who held the premise that "tomorrow will be better." She encouraged my siblings and I to prepare for opportunities and options that were to come.

She fortified her beliefs regarding the future with a never-wavering faith in the power of prayer. Mother's advice on prayer was simple and yet very clear. She said, "When you pray, ask the Lord for health, strength, and wisdom and then get on with what you have to and or need to do!" She was impatient with those who resigned their lives to fate. For her, life's situations were more often than not determined by choices made and/or the path one chooses to travel.

Mother was a proud and courageous woman who measured her success in the distance she traveled throughout her life. She built her life around her family, work, church, and community. She was very proud that all eight of her children finished high school—a personal goal, since there was no public high school for Blacks in our county until 1949. It was a privilege she had been denied growing up in Pittsylvania County, Virginia. Mother touched and improved the lives of others with a kind word, a warm smile, a good meal, and a listening ear.

I learned early from Mother the importance of making wise choices and taking responsibility for choices made. And most importantly, I learned that life is not always easy. By observing the 3 Ps—prayer, perseverance, and preparation—life will get better!

Lesson XXVI:
"The good you do will come back to you"
- DANIEL BOONE ADAMS

Good

   1. a: Something that is good
       b: (1): Something conforming to the moral order of
          the universe
          (2): Praiseworthy character

   2. a: Advancement of prosperity or well-being
       b: Something useful or beneficial

Of all the cherished memories I have retained from my father's challenging discussions around the family dining table, his talks on service to others remain in the forefront of my mind. Dad lived by the motto, "The good you do will come back to you; to your children, and to your children's children."

Mother and Dad believed strongly in the virtue of service and leadership and both of them exemplified this through their work in our community—churches, schools, and neighborhood groups. They offered support, encouragement, and concern for others by giving of themselves freely—time, energy, and resources. Mother and Dad functioned from a posture of moving beyond themselves to help meet the needs of others for the greater good of all.

Dad would often take us with him to perform some service or deed—to assist a neighbor who was ill or behind in handling farming chores; to clean the family church and make it ready for worship services; or to help maintain the community one-room elementary school we all attended.

My mother's life exemplified this one powerful principle. She was a cook by profession and spent her summers during the 50's and early 60's running the dining hall for a girl's camp several miles from our home. (This was during the era of segregation in the south, so all of the girls and camp staff were white). Mother befriended one of the little ten-year old white girls, who hated camp, by allowing her to stay in the kitchen while others went on their daily outings. Years later (1987), Mother suffered a stroke and was taken to the hospital. The doctor on call that day was the little girl from girl's camp who helped save Mother's life. Undoubtedly her fond memories of my mother and her small kindness motivated her to go the extra mile to make sure this good woman stayed around just a while longer. The good you do *will* come back to you.

We're told, "To whom much is given, much is required." Success is not something to hold only unto one's self, but, to be shared with others in the spirit of friendship and compassion.

We introduced the book with the charge that success is an individual quest. We conclude with the challenge that we must use our success to help and serve others.

It is fitting, as we conclude this book of twenty-six "Lessons for Navigating Life," that we end with my father's words, "The good you do will come back to you." These words remind us to live not just for ourselves, but to use our lives as an instrument to reach out and serve others. They point to a higher purpose: to do good work.

Epilogue:
Enjoy the Journey

Life is an adventure, a journey that is worth the trip
- AUTHOR UNKNOWN

Jour·ney
1. An act or instance of traveling from one place to another.
2. Something suggesting travel or passage from one place
   to another.

During seminars, workshops and lectures on "Success," I am frequently asked, "Why make the journey if one is unsure of the destination?" For a response, I look to the late Charles Kuralt (from the CBS news program *Sunday Morning*). Kuralt ended each Sunday Morning's "On the Road" program with the line, "The road up ahead is bending. I wonder what's around the bend." We make the journey to see what's "around the bend."

The fun and fascination of traveling life's journey is the adventure and wonder we experience every day as we ask, "What's around the bend?" It is the bend in the road that gives life its charge, its luster, its mystery, its wonder.

The lessons offered in this book are designed to fortify your resolve to reach the place ahead where the road is bending and to challenge you to maintain the quest to find out for yourself just what lies around that bend.

Let it be a dance we do, May I have this dance with you? In the good times and bad times too, Let it be a dance.

- RIC MASTEN, Singer/Songwriter

And so I challenge you to soak life up! Let the excitement, joy and adventure of discovering your place in time become the very dance of life. Let go of the unfulfilled past and welcome new beginnings. The joy of living is not just hanging on, but actually dancing to the rhythm of life as it evolves. Therefore, if you have a choice, choose to dance! Dance! Dance!

A RECIPE FOR SUCCESS

My high school teacher, Kenneth R. Hannan, made history literally jump off the page. His elegance and eloquence made such an impression on me that I still correspond with him and send annual Christmas cards. He gave our 1958 high school graduating class this "recipe" as a parting gift. I pass it on, now, to you:

INGREDIENTS

4 cups intelligence

1 1/2 cups responsibility

2 cups open-mindedness

1 quart understanding

2 1/2 teaspoons attitude

Dash of judgment

1 1/4 cups sifted initiative

3 cups ambition

2 cups unbeaten patience

1 cup tactfulness

4 cups ability

Have all ingredients at body temperature. Sift Intelligence, Ambition and Understanding together. Mix Cooperation, Attitude and Open-Mindedness until dissolved. Add gradually Ability, Tactfulness and Responsibility. Stir Initiative and Judgment thoroughly. Beat Patience until smooth. Blend all ingredients well; sprinkle liberally with Cheerfulness, and bake in an oven of Determination. When absorbed thoroughly cool and spread with Common Sense.

Yours Always,

Kenneth R. Hennant